American Outlaws: The Lives and Le[

By Charles River E[

About Charles River Editors

Charles River Editors was founded by Harvard and MIT alumni to provide superior editing and original writing services, with the expertise to create digital content for publishers across a vast range of subject matter. In addition to providing original digital content for third party publishers, Charles River Editors republishes civilization's greatest literary works, bringing them to a new generation via ebooks.

Visit charlesrivereditors.com for more information.

Introduction

Bonnie Parker (1910-1934) and Clyde Barrow (1909-1934)

"You've read the story of Jesse James
Of how he lived and died
If you're still in need of something to read
Here's the story of Bonnie and Clyde." – Bonnie Parker, "The Trail's End"

America has always preferred heroes who weren't clean cut, an informal ode to the rugged individualism and pioneering spirit that defined the nation in previous centuries. While the Founding Fathers of the 18th century were revered, the early 19th century saw the glorification of frontier folk heroes like Davy Crockett and Daniel Boone. After the Civil War, the outlaws of the West were more popular than the marshals, with Jesse James and Billy the Kid finding their way into dime novels. And at the height of the Great Depression in the 1930s, there were the "public enemies", common criminals and cold blooded murderers elevated to the level of folk heroes by a public frustrated with their own inability to make a living honestly.

There was no shortage of well known public enemies like John Dillinger and Baby Face Nelson, but none fascinated the American public as much as Bonnie and Clyde. While the duo and their Barrow Gang were no more murderous than other outlaws of the era, the duo's romantic relationship and the discovery of photographs at one of their hideouts added a more human dimension to Bonnie and Clyde, even as they were gunning down civilians and cops alike.

When Bonnie and Clyde were finally cornered and killed in a controversial encounter with police, a fate they shared with many other outlaws of the period, their reputations were cemented. In some way though, the sensationalized version of their life on the run is less interesting than reality, which included actual human drama within the gang.

American Outlaws: The Lives and Legacies of Bonnie and Clyde looks at the lives and crimes of the famous outlaws, but it also humanizes them and examines their relationship. Along with pictures of Bonnie Parker, Clyde Barrow and important people, places, and events in their lives, you will learn about two of America's most notorious outlaws like you never have before, in no time at all.

Chapter 1: A Girl Named Bonnie

"You've heard of a woman's glory
Being spent on a "downright cur"
Still you can't always judge the story
As true, being told by her." – Bonnie Parker, "The Trail's End"

Bonnie and a 1932 Ford V-8 B-400 convertible sedan. The picture was found by lawmen in Joplin while the Barrow Gang was on the run.

Bonnie Elizabeth Parker was born on October 1, 1910 in Rowena, Texas to parents who were a typical middle-class American family of that era. Bonnie was the middle child of the family, along with Buster, who was older than Bonnie, and Billie Jean, who was born two years later. When Bonnie was four, her father Charles died, leaving Bonnie's mother Emma a poor widow with three young children. In order to survive, she left Rowena and moved in with her parents in a Dallas suburb known as Cement City.

From all appearances, Bonnie was a happy, well-adjusted child who did well in school. She won several academic honors in high school and was particularly adept at writing and public speaking. America would soon learn all about her writing abilities, as the outlaw spent some of her time writing poems about her exploits, including the prophetic "The Trail's End," better known as "The Story of Bonnie and Clyde".

In her sophomore year, Bonnie met a rough character named Roy Thornton. Much to her family's dismay she left high school and married him on September 25, 1926, days before her 16th birthday. Not surprisingly, the marriage proved to be a disaster, as Thornton spent much of his time dodging the law and often left his very young wife on her own for days at a time. Bonnie left him in January of 1929 but never filed for divorce. Though Bonnie would forever be associated with another man, she was wearing Thornton's wedding ring when she died, and by that point Thornton was in jail himself. Though they were no longer together, he had followed his wife's exploits with interest and told a reporter ruefully, "I'm glad they went out like they did. It's much better than being caught." Thornton would be killed in an attempted prison escape in 1937.

Thornton

Following her separation from Thornton, Bonnie moved back in with her mother and took a job as a waitress in Dallas. She was a pretty girl at that time. She had an oval face and fair skin, which she accented by bright lipstick. She wore her auburn hair bobbed and curled on the ends. Her thin figure (her wanted poster said she was 5 foot 5 inches tall and weighed only 100 pounds) was well suited for the short, flapper style dresses of the 20s.

One of her most frequent customers was Ted Hinton, a postal worker who would soon join the Dallas Sheriff's Office and, just a few years later, fire some of the bullets that killed her. But that day was still a few years off, and Bonnie was just a friendly young waitress trying to survive in a seedy part of Dallas. She briefly kept a diary during these early years and her turbulent marriage to Thornton, in which she wrote a nearly heart wrenching account of her loneliness, still so young and yet already feeling used up by life:

Dear Diary,

Before opening this year's diary I wish to tell you that I have a roaming husband with a roaming mind. We are separated again for the third and last time. The first time, August 9-19, 1927; and the second time, October 1-19, 1927; and the third time, December 5, 1927. I love him very much and miss him terribly. But I intend doing my duty. I am not going to take him back. I am running around with Rosa Mary Judy and she is somewhat a consolation to me. We have resolved this New Year's to take no men or nothing seriously. Let all men go to hell! But we are not going to sit back and let the world sweep by us.

January 1, 1928. New Year's nite. 12:00 The bells are ringing, the old year has gone, and my heart has gone with it. I have been the happiest and most miserable woman this last year. I wish the old year would have taken my past with it. I mean all my memories, but I can't forget Roy. I am very blue tonight. No word from him. I feel he has gone for good. This is New Years Day, Jan. 1. I went to a show. Saw Ken Maynard in The Overland Stage. Am very blue. Well, I must confess this New Years nite I got drunk, trying to forget. Drowning my sorrows in bottled hell.

January 2, 1928. Met Rosa Mary today and we went to a show. Saw Ronald Coleman and Vilma Banky in A Night Of Love. Sure was a good show. Saw Scottie and gave him the air. He's a pain in the neck to me. Came home at 5:30. went to bed at 10:30. Sure am lonesome."

Her only way out of these feelings of despair lay in regular visits to the local movie theater, where, lost in the dark, she could indulge in dreams of a better, more exciting life. She mentioned some of the movies she saw, including *Framed* (starring Milton Sills), *Afraid to Love* (starring Clive Brook and Florence Vidor), *Marriage* starring (Virginia Valli), and *The Primrose Path* (starring Clara Bow).

Chapter 2: A Boy Named Clyde

> "They call them cold-blooded killers
> They say they are heartless and mean
> But I say this with pride, I once knew Clyde
> When he was honest and upright and clean.
>
> But the laws fooled around and taking him down
> and locking him up in a cell
> 'Til he said to me, "I'll never be free,
> So I'll meet a few of them in hell." – Bonnie Parker, "The Trail's End"

Clyde Chestnut Barrow was born on March 24, 1909 in Ellis County, Texas, joining four older siblings born to Henry Basil and Cumie Walker Barrow. The senior Barrows were poor farmers and would go on to have seven more children before moving, a few at a time, to West Dallas, something of a slum, during the early 1920s. The family was so poor that they spent their first few months in town living under their wagon while saving up money to buy a tent.

In 1926, Clyde, longing to experience the way the "other half" lived, rented a car for a joy ride around the countryside. The problem was he decided not to return it. His mugshot from that incident shows a young, clean cut looking boy of 16, with dark eyes and slightly pointed ears. It looks more like it belongs to a kid running for class treasurer than a future murderer. However, the class treasury was not the money that Clyde wanted to control.

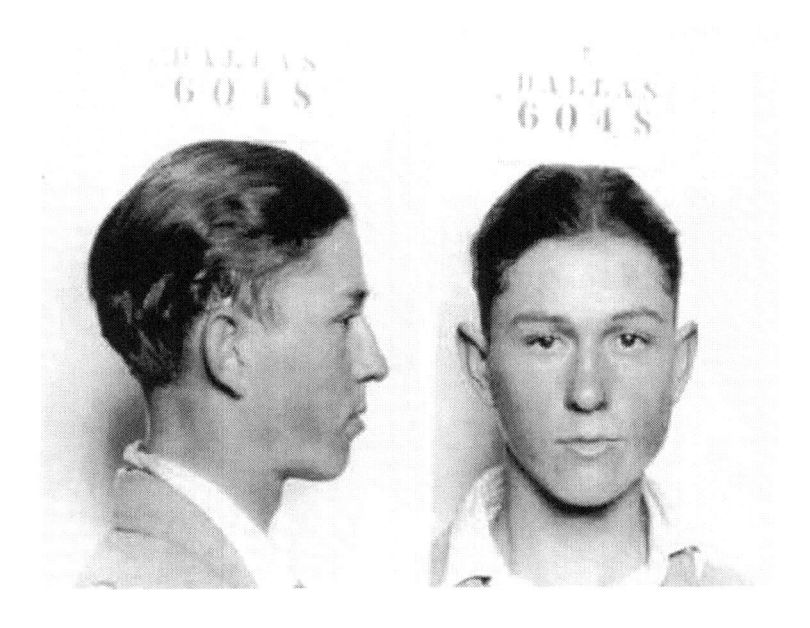

Before many months passed, Clyde was arrested again when he and his brother Buck stole some turkeys. They were not convicted, probably due to their poverty and age, and they soon obtained paying jobs. Nevertheless, they persisted in augmenting their meager honest earnings by stealing cars and robbing stores. As a result, Clyde was arrested several more times until, in April 1930, he was eventually sent to Eastham Prison Farm. Eastham had a reputation throughout the state for its dangerous conditions and heavy workloads. It was designed to punish hardened male criminals by making them spend most of their waking hours working in the hot Texas sun.

For Clyde, it wasn't the hot days that were the problem; it was the dark nights when his cellmate would repeatedly rape him. When he could take the abuse no longer, he beat the man to death, thus committing his first murder at the age of 21. By the time he got out of prison the following year, his own sisters barely recognized the hardened criminal their brother had become. His sister Marie later noted, "Something awful sure must have happened to him in prison, because he wasn't the same person when he got out." That was seconded by Ralph Fults, an inmate at Eastham, who said Clyde changed " from a schoolboy to a rattlesnake."

Chapter 3: The Couple

"The road was so dimly lighted

There were no highway signs to guide
But they made up their minds if all roads were blind
They wouldn't give up 'til they died.

The road gets dimmer and dimmer
Sometimes you can hardly see
But it's fight man to man, and do all you can
For they know they can never be free."

In January 1930, Bonnie lost her job at the diner and left her mother's house to stay with a friend in West Dallas who had a broken arm and needed help around the house. One day, while she was in the kitchen making hot chocolate, there was a knock at the door. Her friend called for the person to come in, and Clyde Barrow stepped into the cramped little living room. Coming out of the kitchen to see who was visiting, Bonnie came face to face with the man of her dreams. Though not yet a hardened criminal, Barrow already had a number of crimes under his belt, and he would soon be sent away to Eastham. While he was gone, Bonnie remained faithful to him, building up in her mind a fantasy of the romantic adventures the two of them would enjoy when he got out.

Thus, she ready to join what became known as "The Barrow Gang," which Clyde formed soon after leaving Eastham in February 1932. Armed with an M1919 Browning Automatic Rifle, Clyde was soon out robbing small grocery stores and gas stations. His goal, along with that of his friend Ralph Fults, was to gather enough money and guns to stage a retaliatory raid on Eastham Prison, whom Clyde held responsible for his sexual assaults and other mistreatment. If they could break out other prisoners, all the better.

Bonnie soon earned her place in the group, being captured on April 19 after a failed burglary against a hardware store. She was kept for a few months in Kaufman County jail in Texas until June 17, when the grand jury decided not to indict her because of her youth and previous clean record. Instead, they released her with a stern warning to stay out of trouble in the future. Instead, she quickly returned to Clyde and a life of crime.

However, Ralph Fults, who had been arrested with her, had been convicted and given a much longer sentence. He was never involved with the gang again, but Bonnie and Clyde carried on without him. By this time, Clyde was wanted for the murder of J. N. Bucher, the owner of a store he robbed in Hillsboro, Texas, on April 30, 1932. In actuality, Clyde was probably an accomplice who waited behind the wheel of the getaway car during that robbery, but he would have plenty of blood on his hands soon enough.

Chapter 4: The Barrow Gang

> "Now Bonnie and Clyde are the Barrow Gang,
> I'm sure you all have read
> how they rob and steal and those who squeal
> are usually found dying or dead.
>
> There's lots of untruths to these write-ups
> They're not so ruthless as that
> Their nature is raw, they hate all law
> Stool pigeons, spotters, and rats."

In August 1932, Bonnie left the gang long enough to visit her mother in Dallas, and while she was gone, Clyde, along with Raymond Hamilton and Ross Dyer, attended a barn dance just across the Texas state line in Stringtown, Oklahoma. They were sitting outside the dance, drinking, when Stringtown Sheriff C. G. Maxwell and his deputy, Eugene Moore, approached them to find out what they were doing. Though there is no evidence to indicate that either man knew anything about who they were, Barrow still saw a uniform, and that's all it took. He and Hamilton fired on both men, killing Moore. Though Maxwell was seriously injured, he was able to survive the attack and describe the two shooters.

High with a sense of having struck out against authority, Barrow quickly attacked again, this time killing a storekeeper who didn't give up the $28 in his cash register quickly enough. This October 11 robbery, which took place in Sherman, Texas, was yet another example of the escalating violence in the gang's tactics.

On Christmas Eve 1932, 16 year old W. D. Jones became the youngest member of the Barrow gang. A family friend for years, Jones already had a criminal record and naturally looked up to the bad boy Clyde and wanted to be like him. He rode out of Dallas with them that night, and in an interview with Playboy decades later, he described what happened on Christmas Day.

I had got with Clyde and Bonnie the night before in Dallas. Me and L. C., that's Clyde's younger brother, was driving home from a dance in his daddy's old car. Here come Bonnie and Clyde. They honked their car horn and we pulled over. I stayed in the car. L. C. got out and went back to see what they wanted. Then he hollered at me, "Hey, come on back. Clyde wants to talk to you." Clyde was wanted then for murder and kidnapping, but I had knowed him all my life. So I got out and went to his car.

He told me, "We're here to see Momma and Marie." (That's Clyde's baby sister.) "You stay with us while L. C. gets them." I was 16 years old and Clyde was only seven years older, but he always called me "Boy."

Them was Prohibition days and about all there was to drink was home-brew. That's what me and L. C. had been drinking that Christmas Eve and it was about all gone. Clyde had some moonshine in his car, so I stayed with him, like he said, while L. C. fetched his folks. They lived just down the road in back of the filling station Old Man Barrow run.

After the visiting was over, Clyde told me him and Bonnie had been driving a long ways and was tired. He wanted me to go with them so I could keep watch while they got some rest. I went. I know now it was a fool thing to do, but then it seemed sort of big to be out with two famous outlaws. I reckoned Clyde took me along because he had knowed me before and figured he could count on me.

It must have been two o'clock Christmas morning when we checked into a tourist court at Temple. They slept on the bed. I had a pallet on the floor.

Next morning, I changed two tires on that Ford Clyde had. Clyde really banked on them Fords. They was the fastest and the best, and he knew bow to drive them with one foot in the gas tank all the time. We went into town and stopped around the comer from a grocery store.

Clyde handed me an old .41-caliber thumb buster and told me, "Take this, boy, and stand watch while I get us some spending money." Later, I found out that gun wouldn't shoot because there was two broken bullets stuck inside the chamber. I had to punch them out with a stick.

I stood outside the store while Clyde went in. Bonnie was waiting in the car around the corner. After he got the money, we walked away toward Bonnie. Now, the blocks in them days was longer than they are now; and before we got halfway back to the car, Clyde stopped alongside a Model A roadster that had the keys in it. I don't know if he'd seen something over his shoulder that spooked him or what. But he told me, "Get in that car, boy, and start it." I jumped to it. But it was a cold day and the car wouldn't start. Clyde got impatient. He told me to slip over and he'd do it. I scooted over. About then an old man and an old woman run over to the roadster and began yelling, "That's my boy's car! Get out!" Then another woman run up and began making a big fuss. All the time, Clyde was trying to get it started. He told them to stand back and they wouldn't get hurt. Then the guy who owned it run up. Clyde pointed his pistol and yelled, "Get back ' man, or I'll kill you." That man was Doyle Johnson, I learned later. He came on up to the car and reached through the roadster's isinglass window curtains and got Clyde by the throat and tried to choke him.

Clyde hollered, "Stop, man, or I'll kill you." Johnson didn't move, and Clyde done what he had threatened. About then he got the car started and we whipped around the corner to where Bonnie was waiting. We piled into her car and lit a shuck out of town.

It all seemed pointless then as to why Clyde wanted that car. I've thought about it since, and I figure he must have wanted the laws to think we was in Johnson's car. Of course, he didn't have no way of knowing he was gonna have to kill Johnson.

We headed out of town toward Waco. A mile or two down the road, Clyde pulled over and said, "Boy, shinny up that pole and cut them phone wires. We don't want no calls ahead." I done it and we went on.

As I look back, cutting them phone wires was slick. That was about all you had to do to cut off the law in them days. There wasn't no two-way radio hookups like now; and when a police used them long-distance phone wires to call the next town, it run up expenses. Them was hard times and even towns didn't have much to spend. There wasn't as many laws then, either, and they just couldn't catch up with Clyde in them V8 Fords he drove. Ted Hinton and Bob Alcorn, the Dallas lawmen I come to know a year later, told me Clyde was about the best driver in the world. They said them Fords and Clyde's driving was what kept him and Bonnie free them two years. Hell, I knowed that. I rode with him. He had me drive some when he was tired, but Clyde stayed behind the' wheel when the heat was close. He believed in a nonstop jump in territory -- sometimes as much as 1000 miles --whenever it got hot behind. He and Bonnie didn't in- tend to ever be taken alive. They was hell-bent on running till the end, and they knowed there was only one end for them. Sometimes I thought Clyde liked the running. He dreaded getting caught, but he never give up robbing to work for a living. I reckon Clyde just didn't want to work like other folks. For one thing, he never liked getting his hands dirty.

27 year old Doyle Johnson was a new father who was on his way home for Christmas dinner. Though Jones claimed Clyde shot Johnson, accounts of the shooting claimed the firing came from the passenger side, implicating Jones. According to Jones, those accounts gave Clyde all he needed to ensure Jones had to stay with the gang, and Clyde told the youngster, "Boy, you can't go home. You got murder on you, just like me."

Regardless of who pulled the trigger, the pair stole Johnson's car and drove it to Tarrant County, where, two weeks later, they killed Deputy Sheriff Malcolm Davis. Like Doyle Johnson, Davis was in the wrong place at the wrong time. He had been staking out a quiet part of town waiting for another wanted criminal when Clyde and Jones came upon the scene accidentally. The murder of Deputy Sheriff Davis was Clyde's 5th killing since his February 1932 release, and he had been involved in the grave wounding of another officer as well.

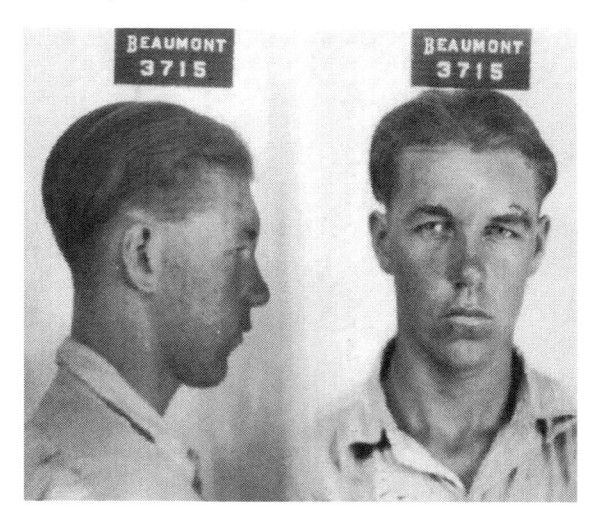

1931 mugshot of 15 year old William Daniel Jones. Jones and his friend L.C. Barrow were arrested after stealing and crashing a car.

In late March 1933, Clyde's brother Buck was finally released from prison after having been given a full pardon by the governor of Texas. He and his wife, Blanche, moved in with Bonnie, Clyde and Jones at 3347 ½ Oakridge Drive in Joplin, Missouri. They lived a quiet life and might well indeed have escaped notice and arrest but for the group's insistence on regularly hosting noisy card games that went until all hours of the night and were fueled by the newly legalized beer available with the end of Prohibition. The group routinely went through as much as a case of beer each evening, and during one particularly rowdy party, Clyde accidentally shot off his rifle, causing the neighbors to complain to the local police force.

Buck and Blanche Barrow

Believing that they were only dealing with a bunch of rowdy citizens, five police officers surrounded the garage apartment on April 13, 1933, but when they called for those inside to come out with their hands up, everyone except Blanch came out shooting. They killed Detective McGinnis on the spot, while Constable Harryman later died of his wounds. Then, with Bonnie providing cover fire, the men jumped in the car and got it started. They swung by to grab Bonnie and then headed down the street after Blanche, who had gone after Snow Ball, her little white dog.

The Joplin hideout

When the dust settled, one officer had a face full of splinters from wood thrown at him by Bonnie's shooting, one officer was dead, another was dying and two had escaped uninjured. Of the gang, young Jones was the most seriously injured, having been shot in the side. Buck was bleeding from where a ricocheted bullet grazed him and Clyde had a bullet hole in his suitcase.

What the group left behind proved to be much more important to the legend than anything they took with them. The police found confirming evidence of all involved, including Buck and Blanche Barrow's marriage license, as well as his three week old parole papers. They also found a significant collection of guns and a camera with several rolls of undeveloped film. Most interesting of all, they found the poem "Suicide Sal," which had been written by Bonnie.

16 year old W.D. Jones posing

Because they had no photo lab of their own, the police took the film to the local paper, *The Joplin Globe*, for development. As a result, a full page story soon ran featuring a cigar smoking Bonnie holding a pistol, Clyde and Buck playing around while pointing guns at each other, a host of other salacious pictures of the two couples, and Bonnie's poem "Suicide Sal." The newly formed newswire service picked up the story, and "The Barrow Gang" became front page news all over the country. Jones explained the origins of the photos that made the gang famous:

> Bonnie smoked cigarettes, but that cigar bit folks like to tell about is phony. I guess I got that started when. I gave her my cigar to hold when I was making her picture. I made most of them pictures the laws picked up when we fled Joplin, Missouri, leaving

everything in the apartment except the guns. I seen a lot of them pictures in the newspapers afterward -- Them little poems Bonnie made up made the papers, too. She would think up rhymes in her head and put them down on paper when we stopped. Some of them she kept, but she threw a lot of them away.

Chapter 5: Celebrities

Bonnie and Clyde were probably certain of their ultimate fate, but they almost certainly relished their fame and publicity at the same time. In April 1934, Henry Ford received a letter purportedly authored by Clyde thanking the famous car maker for producing Clyde's favorite kind of car:

Mr. Henry Ford

Detroit Mich.

Dear Sir: --

While I still have got breath in my lungs I will tell you what a dandy car you make. I have drove Fords exclusively when I could get away with one. For sustained speed and freedom from trouble the Ford has got ever other car skinned and even if my business hasen't been strickly legal it don't hurt anything to tell you what a fine car you got in the V8 --

Yours truly

Clyde Champion Barrow

While it's still unclear whether Clyde actually wrote that letter, historians and analysts believe that the spelling errors can be explained by his lack of education, and there's no doubt Clyde was a big fan of the V-8. Others believe that the handwriting of the letter resemble Bonnie's handwriting. Of course, if Clyde didn't author it, the letter was a clear example of Clyde's notoriety, and a short time afterward Ford received a letter purported to be from John Dillinger (though the Dillinger letter was later proven to be a fraud).

However, the publicity came at a cost. With the published photos plastering their faces on newspapers across the nation, it became more and more dangerous for anyone from the gang to appear in public. For that reason, the gang was constantly on the move, and over the next three months they worked their way from Texas to Minnesota, stopping along the way in Lucerne, Indiana in May to try to rob a bank. Though they failed in that job, they succeeded a little while later in Okabena, Minnesota. As a result of their frequent travels, the Barrow Gang got credit for crimes they didn't actually commit, while false sightings in places they were far away from also became common. Jones recounted one example:

> Some of the tales about us robbing banks all the time ain't true, either. The time I was with Clyde and Bonnie, we never made a bank job. He liked grocery stores, filling stations and places there was a payroll. Why should we rob a bank? There was never much money in the banks back in them days in the Southwest. But that's not the way the papers put it. They'd write we was heisting a bank in Texas when we was actually off in Tennessee or somewhere else. I remember one time we stopped at a tourist court in a little town. I went across the road to an inn to get some sandwiches. The waiter was all excited. "Bonnie and Clyde was just here," he told me. "They stopped for gas. The police come out, but they got here too late. Bonnie and Clyde was already gone and they couldn't catch them." It shook me some when he said that, but I stayed calm.

> I took the food back to the tourist cabin and told Clyde what the man had said. He got a good laugh out of that, but after we had eat, he said, "You know, that man might have been giving us a tip. He might have recognized us. We better move on."

Eventually, Henry Methvin had joined the gang, and Methvin would prove to be the "weak link" in the chain that would eventually break.

```
HENRY METHVIN.
Age 20 (1931).Ht 5-9½ Wt 170. Hair Lt.Brown
Eyes blue. Complex Fair. Marks and scars.
1 dim horizontal cut scar left middle
finger 1st joint 2 dagger pierced and
lettered "love" right forearm inner.
```

Methvin's mugshot

While the American public was fascinated by the notion of young lovers on the run, the Barrow Gang faced a much starker reality. Because they now lived in constant fear of being recognized, the Barrow Gang no longer ate in restaurants or slept in motels. Instead, they camped in the woods outside of towns, cooked their meals over make shift fires and bathed in cold, shallow streams. On top of all that, the gang constantly had to steal new cars. As Jones later explained:

Clyde drove most always, 'cause he didn't trust nobody else to drive like he could. As for me working on the car, I'd change a tire or a battery or something like that. But we'd junk a car if anything went wrong with it and get another one. I don't know how many cars I stole for Clyde. I do remember we never kept one more than a week or so, because it'd get too hot…

We never stayed long in one place. It was too risky. We had to keep moving. When our clothes got dirty, we'd take them to a cleaners if we thought it was safe. But we didn't wait until they was ready. We'd drive on somewhere else and, in a week or two, swing back to pick them up, if there was no heat behind. Sometimes we never got back. We'd buy new clothes.

Any shopping we done was done alone. Me and Clyde would wait in the car down the street while Bonnie went in and got what she wanted. Or he would go in a store while we waited out in the car.

I always figured some of them reporters was holed up somewhere with some booze during the time they claimed they'd been off with the law in hot pursuit of the outrageous Barrow gang. They was just writing from their imagination, it seemed to me. I couldn't read what they was saying in the papers then, but we'd pick up the newspaper in whatever little town we was traveling through and Bonnie would read it aloud. That way, we kept up with where the law thought we was and we'd head in the opposite direction.

These conditions, along with the fact that the five members spent most of their days riding around in cars lacking air conditioning, made life very unpleasant for everyone. Jones noted that the passengers often rode for hours in complete silence:

There was never a whole lot of talk among us when we was on the road. Often what seemed like hours of silence would be broken as Clyde looked at her and said something like, "Honey, _ as soon as I find a place, I'm gonna stop. I'm tired and want to get some rest." He always called her "Honey" or "Baby" and she called him "Daddy" or "Honey." They called me "Boy." I got to where I called Bonnie "Sis" and Clyde "Bud." We couldn't say each other's names, because somebody at a filling station or a tourist court might pick up on them and call, the 'law.

Bonnie was always agreeable with Clyde, but they did have some fallings out. I've seen them fall out over a can of sardines. He jerked it out of her hands and opened it with his pocketknife, and her trying to tell him it had an opener. But I never heard them call each other bad names. They hardly ever used dirty words. I've heard today's teenagers use words worse than Clyde and Bonnie, and they was deadly outlaws.

Sometimes, when she got puffed up about something, Clyde would kid her and say, "Why don't you go on home to Momma, baby? You probably wouldn't get more than ninety-nine years. Texas hasn't sent a woman to the chair yet, and I'd send in my recommendation for leniency." She'd laugh at him then and everything would be smooth again.

Jones ultimately reached the point that he couldn't stand the confinement anymore and stole a car to get away from everyone. However, the loneliness soon changed his mind, and he returned to the gang on June 8, 1933.

Two days later, perhaps while drinking, arguing or both, Clyde flipped the car that he, Bonnie and Jones were riding in. While he and Jones walked away unscathed, Bonnie's leg was very badly burned. The two men managed to get Bonnie to a nearby farm, where a Mrs. Pritchard examined the leg, saw that it was burned to the bone near the knee and insisted that they needed to call a doctor. When Clyde seemed reluctant, Mr. Pritchard became suspicious and slipped away to call the police. Upon noticing his host was missing, Clyde picked up the crying Bonnie and, with Jones on his heels, ran out the door, jumping in Pritchard's car and driving away.

From there they drove to Fort Smith, Arkansas, where they got a room in a tourist court. Clyde finally agreed to bring in a doctor, who insisted that Bonnie needed round the clock nursing. Unable to risk taking her to a hospital, he hired a private nurse to care for her. He also contacted Bonnie's sister, Billie Jean, who travelled from Texas to help care for her sister.

In need of quick money, Buck Barrow and Jones attempted and failed to rob a local bank in Alma, Arkansas, killing Marshal Henry Humphrey in the process. This brought out every lawman in the area, and forced the group to go on the run again, dragging the nearly delirious Bonnie with them. According to Jones, "Bonnie never got over that burn. Even after it healed over, her leg was drawn under her. She had to just hop or hobble along. When she was so bad at first, we had to carry her to the toilet and take her off when she finished and put her back in bed.

Chapter 6: The Manhunt

> "If a policeman is killed in Dallas
> And they have no clue or guide
> If they can't find a fiend, just wipe the slate clean
> And hang it on Bonnie and Clyde.
>
> There's two crimes committed in America
> Not accredited to the Barrow Mob
> They had no hand in the kidnap demand
> Nor the Kansas City Depot job."

The Red Crown Tourist Court

The gang's next stop was the Red Crown Tourist Court in Platte City, Missouri, where they rented both the small brick cabins available on July 19, 1933. Unbeknownst to them, the tavern by the same name, located just across the street, was a favorite hang-out for Missouri Highway Patrolmen. Still, had they behaved themselves, they might have avoided notice, but just like in Joplin, the Barrow Gang proved incapable of avoiding notice.

Blanche made the first mistake by strolling into the tourist court office wearing riding breeches and registering only three people. The owner of the tourist court, Neal Houser, knew that the average woman driving with her family through Missouri did not wear riding breeches. On top of that, when he looked out the window, he saw clearly that more than three people were getting out of the car, including what appeared to be crippled women being carried. Furthermore, Houser also noticed that they backed their car into the driveway, as if ready to make a quick get-away. The gang also paid for both their lodging and five meals each day with coins instead of bills, and with all that Houser was thoroughly suspicious. However, the icing on the cake was that they covered all the windows, which were already curtained, with sheets of newspaper. Houser decided to stroll across the street and mention his unusual guests to one of the Highway Patrolmen, Captain William Baxter, who was drinking coffee at the tavern.

In the meantime, local Sheriff Holt Coffey received word that the infamous Bonnie had been injured and that the gang was on the run again. So when the local druggist called and told him about some suspicious looking characters who had come by to purchase bandages and atropine sulfate (used for treating burns), he decided to put a man near the tourist court to see what was going on. He also contacted Baxter, who agreed that this might be the real deal. Together they planned a raid, sending to nearby Kansas City for reinforcements and an armored car.

The same night the gang arrived, at 11:00 p.m., Coffey, Baxter and their men surrounded the cabins, sending an officer to bang on the door and order everyone out. Instead, all three men began firing out the doors and windows. Much to the gang's surprise, the "local yokels" they expected returned fire with submachine guns, forcing them to take cover on the floor. Buck, refusing to take cover, attempted to fire back and was hit in the head by two rounds.

Clyde carried the unconscious Bonnie to the garage and threw her in the back seat of the car while Jones checked outside for an escape route. Clyde went back and grabbed Buck while Jones fired on the armored car blocking them in. The driver pulled out of the line of fire, allowing the gang to shoot its way out and escape. During the chaos, Jones had been shot in the shoulder, and Blanche had been blinded by shards of glass that struck her in both eyes.

With four moaning, injured people in the car, Clyde drove through the dark night. Five days later they made camp in a disused amusement park in Dexter, Iowa, but their presence was soon noted by local citizens, who alerted the police. This time, the police called on every man in the community who could fire a gun to help surround the five and open fire. While Bonnie, Clyde and Jones were able to escape, they left the dying Buck behind, along with Blanche. Buck died a few days later, and Blanche was later convicted as an accessory to murder and served ten years in prison.

The arrest of Blanche Barrow

Still determined to live long enough to complete his revenge, Clyde dragged the injured Bonnie and W.D. northwest to Colorado, then back to Minnesota and then south again to Mississippi, pulling mostly small jobs so that they had spending money. One notable exception was when the three robbed the armory in Plattville, Illinois, taking with them three new Browning Automatic Rifles, a number of handguns and as much ammunition as they could carry.

After six weeks on the run, the trio returned to Dallas in September to visit their families. It seems that by now Bonnie and Clyde knew that the end was near, and in a way the trip seemed like one last chance to come home to say good bye. By now, Jones had had enough, and he left with their permission to visit his mother and not return:

> I left Clyde and Bonnie after they was healed up enough to get by without me. Clyde put me out to steal a car and I hooked 'em back to Texas.

> I'd had enough blood and hell.

> But it wasn't done yet. I had to pay. A boy in Houston, where I was working for a vegetable peddler, knowed me and turned me in to the law. They tried me for killing a

sheriff's man at Dallas. Clyde done it, but I was glad to take the rap. Arkansas wanted to extradite me, and. I sure didn't want to go to no Arkansas prison. I figure now that if Arkansas had got me, one of them skeletons they've dug up there might have been me.

As Jones indicated, he was quickly arrested in Houston, on November 16. He would hear about the final demise of Bonnie and Clyde from a jail cell.

Leaving Bonnie with her family, Clyde went about the Texas countryside, executing small time robberies with the help of local hoodlums who were excited to get to pull a job with the notorious Clyde Barrow. On November 22, he took Bonnie with him to Sowers, Texas to visit some more family members, but Dallas Sheriff Smoot Schmid got wind of their plans and ambushed the two, firing on their car. While they got away, they were both shot in the legs by a single bullet from a BAR. A few days later, a Dallas grand jury would finally indict Bonnie for the murder of Deputy Malcolm Davis. Though Bonnie was often portrayed in the media as the mastermind and the cold-blooded killer in the group, Jones claimed that it was quite the opposite: "Bonnie was the only one Clyde trusted all the way. But not even Bonnie had a voice in the decisions. His leadership was undisputed. She always agreed with him when he ' hinted he might like to hear her advice on something. As far as I know, Bonnie never packed a gun. Maybe she'd help carry what we had in the car into a tourist-court room. But during the five big gun battles I was with them, she never fired a gun. But I'll say she was a hell of a loader."

The two spent the month of December laying low, perhaps hoping to spend what they might have sensed would be their last Christmas quietly. However, they started 1934 off with a bang, both literally and figuratively, when Clyde finally attacked the Eastham State Prison. On January 16 he sprung his friends Raymond Hamilton and Henry Methvin from the hell-hole that had been the source of so much of his pain. In the process, he killed a prison officer, Major Joe Crowson.

There is a reason for the old saying "don't mess with Texas" and Clyde's attack on the prison brought the force of the entire Lone Star State down on his head, in addition to all the federal officials who were already looking for him. The Texas Department of Corrections brought one of the most famous Texas Rangers in history, Captain Frank A. Hamer, out of retirement to go after what was left of the Barrow Gang. Hamer was the perfect man for the job, unafraid to kill anyone that might harm a fellow Texan. According to his record, he had personally sent more than 50 criminals to their graves and had been wounded 17 times in the process. Unlike some others in the organization, he made it clear that he would have no problem firing on Bonnie Parker, even though she was a woman.

Beginning on February 10, 1934, Hamer had one purpose: capture Bonnie and Clyde, dead or alive.

Hamer

Chapter 7: Public Reaction

>From heartbreak some people have suffered
>From weariness some people have died
>But all in all, our troubles are small
>'Til we get like Bonnie and Clyde.
>
>A newsboy once said to his buddy
>"I wish old Clyde would get jumped
>In these hard times we's get a few dimes
>If five or six cops would get bumped."

In many ways it's impossible today for cold-blooded cop killers to become folk heroes, but there were several extenuating circumstances about Depression Era America that made it possible. First, when Bonnie and Clyde first came on the scene in 1932, the American people were still smarting from what they perceived to be a betrayal of their hopes and dreams. The fathers of middle class families had lived through a World War with the promise that, once the Kaiser was beat, all would be well. They had returned home to hope for a secure future based on hard work and careful saving. The Financial Crash of 1929 had smashed their hopes to pieces and left most of them even poorer than when they had started. In the secret places that they would not admit, perhaps not even to themselves, Clyde's reign of terror against the established systems seemed a little like sweet revenge.

On the other hand, Bonnie's devil may care attitude had a certain attraction for the hardworking housewife. Like Bonnie, they had once been free to stay up late and bob their hair. They had traded that for the promise of romantic and financial security. Many a 30 year old woman with four or five children to feed had only just a few years earlier been a prosperous bride with the world at her feet. She and her husband had anticipated only continued prosperity, thanks to a booming economy and cheap land. Then the bank foreclosed and they traded their little house with a picket fence for a shack in the Dust Bowl or a one room walk-up on the backside of a tenement. For some of these women, when Bonnie took a shot at one man who stood between her and what she wanted, she was taking a shot at all the men who had ever let some woman down.

Then, of course, there was the way the papers of the day spun the stories. While reporters did mention the murders, they also told fascinating tales of victims kidnapped by the gang only to be turned loose a few hours or days later with money to get home with. Some of these victims even spoke well of their captors, referring to their good looks or polite manners.

However, any good opinion the public had quickly evaporated on April 1, 1934. That day, Easter Sunday, the gang killed two highway patrolmen, H.D. Murphy and Edward Wheeler, in Grapevine, Texas. Though Methvin fired the first shot, and he later claimed Bonnie walked up to the officer with the intention of helping, rumors flew around the country that she had not only fired on the officers, but that she had stood laughing over the dead officer's body. Others claimed that she left behind a cigar butt with her own teeth marks on it. By the time it was later reported that Bonnie had nothing to do with this shooting, and may have even been passed out pain killers, their public reputation was tarnished.

There was something about this attack that seemed worse to the public. Maybe it was that it happened on what, to most of the country, was one of the most sacred days of the year. Maybe it was because Murphy's young bride-to-be attended his funeral in her wedding gown. Whatever the reason, the public was now thoroughly incensed at the lawlessness around them and wanted it stopped. The Highway Patrol and the governor's office offered a combined reward of $2,000 for the bodies of gang, but specifically for Bonnie and Clyde.

Either unaware of or unconcerned about their new level of notoriety, Clyde and Methvin gunned down 60 year old Constable Cal Campbell five days later just outside of Commerce, Oklahoma. On the same day, they kidnapped the town police chief, Percy Boyd, and then turned him loose with a clean shirt and money to get home with. According to Boyd, Bonnie asked that he tell the world she did not smoke cigars. It seems that of all the things that paper was accusing her of, that was the one that bothered her most.

With Boyd's eyewitness testimony to Campbell's murder, the Oklahoma authorities were able to issue warrants for the arrest of Clyde Barrow and Bonnie Parker specifically. On the other hand, they merely referred to Methvin as "John Doe." This marked the first time that Bonnie was actually seen shooting someone.

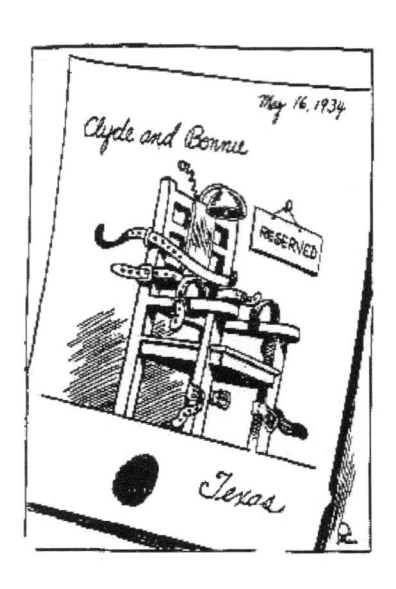

Chapter 8: The Inevitable

> "They don't think they're tough or desperate
> They know the law always wins
> They've been shot at before, but they do not ignore
> That death is the wages of sin.
>
> Some day they'll go down together
> And they'll bury them side by side
> To few it'll be grief, to the law a relief
> But it's death for Bonnie and Clyde."

Beginning with his appointment to the case on February 10, Frank Hamer stalked every move that the remaining Barrow Gang made. One of the things he discovered was that they tended to move in a circular pattern along the states lines of Texas, Louisiana, Arkansas, Oklahoma and Kansas. By moving along state lines, they were able to avoid capture by local officers or highway patrolmen who could not cross state lines. Another thing that he noticed was that the gang tended to visit their families at regular intervals. According to his calculations, the next family due for a visit was Methvin's family in Louisiana.

Because he had a set pattern of behavior, Hamer was able to anticipate his next move and plan accordingly. In mid-May, 1934, Hamer requisitioned a large number of Browning Automatic Rifles and 20 rounds of armor piercing bullets. Then, on May 21, he left Texas with four hand-picked posse members and traveled to Shreveport, Louisiana. There they waited until word reached them through their sources that the trio were heading to Bienville Parish. The three gang members agreed that, in case they became separated, they would meet on an abandoned stretch of highway near Methvin's parents' home. Methvin's father became aware of this arrangement and, under increased pressure from the police, exchanged the information for a promise that his son would not receive the death penalty if captured.

The posse: standing: Ted Hinton, Prentiss Oakley, Manny Gault; seated: Bob Alcorn, Henderson Jordan and Hamer.

Hamer had chosen his posse well. In addition to himself, there was Ted Hinton, who knew Bonnie from her waitressing days, as well as Bob Alcorn, who knew Clyde on sight. There was also former Ranger Manny Gaul, Sheriff Henderson Jordan from Bienville, and his deputy, Prentiss Oakley. Together the men waited outside the rendezvous point on Highway 154 for the little group to show up.

At about 9:00 on the morning of May 23, 1934, the waiting posse heard a car fast approaching. Looking through the bushes they quickly identified it as the stolen Ford that Clyde had last been seen driving. It pulled up alongside Ivan Methvin's truck, placed there by Hamer to attract Clyde's attention and to place his car in the best position for the ambush. The five officers opened fire, spraying the Ford and its occupants with approximately 130 rounds of ammunition. According to interviews with Alcorn and Hinton:

> It was about 9 a. m., when we finally sighted the car. It was a gray V-8 coach, and that was the car we were looking for. We had been waiting at the top of a steep hill, and the car had to slow down as it neared the top. There wasn't any time to think. We didn't have a minute to wonder if we were coming out alive. The name Clyde Barrow and all the terror and danger it involved didn't mean a thing. There were two people in that car and they probably were Clyde and Bonnie. And that car was getting nearer.

There must have been a signal given, but "who it came from is another thing. We just all acted together, stepped out into the road and raised our guns. We all yelled "Halt!" at once.

They didn't halt. The car was going slowly and Clyde let go of the wheel. We could see him grab at a gun in his lap. Bonnie was going for something on the other side.

Then all hell broke loose. There were six men shooting at once. Machine guns? No, thank God. We had shotguns and Browning automatics. We had tried machine guns once before....

You couldn't hear any one shot. It was just a roar, a continuous roar, and it kept up for several minutes. We emptied our guns, reloaded and kept shooting. No chances with Clyde and Bonnie.

As we jumped into sight, I could see Clyde reaching as if to get his gun. But he never had a chance to fire a shot. Neither did Bonnie, though we learned a few minutes later that they both were carrying rifles across their laps.

Each of us six officers had a shotgun and an automatic rifle and pistols.

We opened fire with the automatic rifles. They were emptied before the car got even with us. Then we used shotguns.

After shooting the shotguns, we emptied the pistols at the car, which had passed us and ran into a ditch about 50 yards on down the road. It almost turned over. We kept shooting at the car even after it stopped. We weren't taking any chances.

There was smoke coming from the car, and it looked like it was on fire. I guess this was caused when one of the shotguns Clyde or Bonnie had across their laps went off. They did not have time to raise their guns, but the tightening of their muscles as they were filled with lead might have pressed the trigger. The blast at close range almost tore off ...the door.

We all ran up to the car. Ted opened the door on Bonnie's side and she almost fell out.

She was sitting with her head down between her knees, bent over the gun that was in her lap. Her right hand had been shot away. She was also shot in the mouth, and I learned later that there were about 40 other bullet holes in her.

The door on Clyde's side would not open. His head was hanging out the window.

He too had a shotgun across his lap and a pistol in his hand. The back of his head was shot off.

Bob knew right away that we had at last got the right ones. He knew Clyde when the punk was stealing automobiles. He also knew Bonnie, who used to be a waitress near the courthouse. You can imagine how we felt. Our first thought was to tell the boss, Sheriff Smoot Schmid so we got to the nearest town as quickly as we could and telephoned.

"Did you sleep good last night?" Ted asked Smoot. "No, I didn't." he answered. "Well, you can go on home and sleep now." Ted told him. "We just killed em both." Smoot dropped the phone. Oakley meanwhile went back to Arcadia for the coroner. In the back of the car we found three machine rifles, two automatic shotguns, 10 automatic pistols and 1500 rounds of ammunition. There were a couple of magazines, a detective and a love story. In the seat beside Clyde and Bonnie was a bacon and lettuce sandwich.

Before we got back to the car, however, people just sprang up from everywhere.

Without removing the bodies, we hitched the car onto the back of a truck and towed it into Arcadia, where the bodies were taken to the undertakers. That little town was filled with cars and people.

Among the people who "sprang from everywhere" were women who tried to cut of locks of Bonnie's hair and pieces of her dress. Another man tried to cut off Clyde's trigger finger while another went after his left ear. According to the official coroner's report, Clyde was shot 17 times and Bonnie 26. Each had several headshots, any one of which would have killed them instantly. The undertaker reported having difficulty embalming the body because they were too full of holes to hold the embalming fluid.

Among the 12,000 people that rushed into the little town in the hopes of seeing a piece of history was one lone farmer with a sad, weather beaten face. Henry Barrow had been called in by the police to make an official identification of what was left of his son's body. Afterwards he sat alone in the back of the furniture store where the bodies had been taken and wept. There was also a young man in his mid-20s, dress in a quiet suit. He was Buster Parker, and he was there to bring his sister's body home.

Another person called in that day to help confirm the identities of the dead was H. D. Darby. The previous year, Bonnie and Clyde had stolen his car and kidnapped him and his girlfriend. Giddy and talkative with excitement, Bonnie had asked him what he did for a living. When he replied that he was an undertaker, she cackled with laughter and observed that perhaps one day he'd get to work on her. In fact he did, assisting Mr. McClure of McClure's Funeral Parlor with preparing her body for burial.

Like their short lives, Bonnie and Clyde's respective funerals got completely out of hand. Bonnie's funeral, held at the McCamy-Campbell Funeral Home in Dallas, was inundated with flowers, including arrangements that allegedly came from other "public enemies" such as John Dillinger and Pretty Boy Floyd. However, no bouquet was a large as the one from a group of Dallas news boys, who paid tribute to the woman whose death had allowed them to sell more than half a million papers in one day. 20,000 people showed up at the Fishtrap Cemetery for her burial, making it nearly impossible for the family to get to the gravesite.

Clyde's funeral was private and held at the chapel of the Sparkman-Holtz-Brand Funeral Home in Dallas. He was buried in the Western Heights Cemetery, next to his brother, Buck. A single head stone marks both their graves and says, simply, "gone but not forgotten," just as Clyde had earlier requested.

While this epitaph could not be more appropriate (no one who hears his story will ever forget Clyde Barrow,) it also could not be more poignant. As a young man, he was the fifth of a large, very poor family where there appears to have never been enough of anything, including attention, to go around. Desperate for adventure and money, he made the poor choice of breaking the law. However, the law in turn broke him. The cruelty of the Texas penitentiary system at that time turned a wayward boy into a hardened criminal, and the crimes perpetrated against him while he was in custody played a role in creating Clyde the murderer.

And what of Bonnie? What made a good student turn into a bad moll? For her, it seems that she never overcame the loss of her father at such an age. Good grades may have been her way of gaining family approval and affection until peer acceptance became more important. Then her bad marriage, built on the hope of finally having a man to count on soured her to the possibility of ever being a fully functioning adult and drove her instead toward a life of doing whatever felt good at the moment. She attached herself fully to Clyde, and when it became clear that he would likely die in a hail of bullets, she determined she wanted nothing less than that for herself. In the end, they both got what they wanted.

Chapter 9: The Legend of Bonnie and Clyde

To an extent, the deaths of Bonnie and Clyde signaled the apex of the "Public Enemies Era", and in the next few months, Dillinger, Baby Face Nelson and Pretty Boy Floyd would all be shot dead as well. To help prevent more public enemies, the federal government stepped up their efforts by making bank robbery and kidnapping federal offenses, thus allowing the FBI to get involved in those kinds of crimes.

By then, of course, Bonnie and Clyde had become legends, and their romance, whirlwind lives and ultimate fates made their story a natural on the silver screen. Within decades, Hollywood had depicted their story several times, books had been written, and musicians wrote songs referencing them. In 1967, Warren Beatty and Faye Dunaway added their starpower and striking good looks to the outlaws.

While their story is certainly worth telling, though perhaps not in the sensationalized, romantic way the criminals are often depicted, the portrayals of Bonnie and Clyde are (not surprisingly) often at odds with reality. Far from being swashbuckling, W.D. Jones described Clyde as a young, serious man with a small build:

I was in the joint when word came on May 23, 1934, that Clyde and Bonnie was killed near Arcadia, Louisiana. I've heard stories since that Clyde was homosexual, or, as they say in the pen, a "punk," but they ain't true. Maybe it was Clyde's quiet, polite manner and his slight build that fooled folks.

He was only about five feet, six inches tall and he weighed no more than 135 pounds. Me and him was about the same size, and we used to wear each other's clothes. Clyde had dark hair that was wavy. He never had a beard. Even when he didn't shave, all he had on his chin was fuzz.

Another way that story might have got started was his wearing a wig sometimes when him and Bonnie had to drive through a town where they might be recognized. He wore the wig for disguise and for no other reason.

Clyde never walked right, either. He'd chopped off his big toe and part of the second toe on his left foot when he was in prison, because he couldn't keep up, with the pace the farm boss set.

Or the story could have come from sensation writers who believed anything dropped on them and who blew it to proportions that suited their imagination.

Jones also described Clyde as both polite and even not above praying:

Clyde had good manners, just naturally. It fooled lots of folks, like that policeman in Missouri. We was driving over a bridge and the motor law rolled up beside us and told us to pull over, Clyde smiled and told him, "Just a minute, sir."

It was night and Clyde wanted to get off that bridge before he stopped. But that policeman come on real nasty. "Stop right here now," he said.

Clyde kept right on going and saying, "Just a minute, sir." When we got off the bridge, Clyde turned up a little street and stopped. The policeman come up to the door. That's when Clyde throwed that little shotgun in his face, and that law done a turn around.

Clyde liked to stay sharp and would sometimes hit the car brakes of a sudden, bounce out to the roadside and open up with that cutoff automatic rifle on a tree or a sign for practice. He was never more than an arm's reach from a gun, even in bed, or out of bed on the floor in the night, when he thought we was all asleep and couldn't see him kneeling there. I seen it more than once. He prayed. I reckon he was praying for his soul. Maybe it was for more life. He knowed it would end soon, but he didn't intend for it to be in jail.

Fittingly, it was Jones who dispelled much of the myth-making surrounding the two in his interview with Playboy shortly after the popular 1967 movie about Bonnie and Clyde. "That Bonnie and Clyde movie made it all look sort of glamorous, but like I told them teenaged boys sitting near me at the drive-in showing: 'Take it from an old man who was there. It was hell.'"

Clyde and Jones

The Trail's End

You've read the story of Jesse James
of how he lived and died.
If you're still in need;
of something to read,
here's the story of Bonnie and Clyde.

Now Bonnie and Clyde are the Barrow gang
I'm sure you all have read.
how they rob and steal;
and those who squeal,
are usually found dying or dead.

There's lots of untruths to these write-ups;
they're not as ruthless as that.
their nature is raw;
they hate all the law,
the stool pidgeons, spotters and rats.

They call them cold-blooded killers
they say they are heartless and mean.
But I say this with pride
that I once knew Clyde,
when he was honest and upright and clean.

But the law fooled around;
kept taking him down,
and locking him up in a cell.
Till he said to me;
"I'll never be free,
so I'll meet a few of them in hell"

The road was so dimly lighted
there were no highway signs to guide.
But they made up their minds;
if all roads were blind,
they wouldn't give up till they died.

The road gets dimmer and dimmer
sometimes you can hardly see.
But it's fight man to man
and do all you can,
for they know they can never be free.

From heart-break some people have suffered

from weariness some people have died.
But take it all in all;
our troubles are small,
till we get like Bonnie and Clyde.

If a policeman is killed in Dallas
and they have no clue or guide.
If they can't find a fiend,
they just wipe their slate clean
and hang it on Bonnie and Clyde.

There's two crimes committed in America
not accredited to the Barrow mob.
They had no hand;
in the kidnap demand,
nor the Kansas City Depot job.

A newsboy once said to his buddy;
"I wish old Clyde would get jumped.
In these awfull hard times;
we'd make a few dimes,
if five or six cops would get bumped"

The police haven't got the report yet
but Clyde called me up today.
He said,"Don't start any fights;
we aren't working nights,
we're joining the NRA."

From Irving to West Dallas viaduct
is known as the Great Divide.
Where the women are kin;
and the men are men,
and they won't "stool" on Bonnie and Clyde.

If they try to act like citizens
and rent them a nice little flat.
About the third night;
they're invited to fight,
by a sub-gun's rat-tat-tat.

They don't think they're too smart or desperate
they know that the law always wins.
They've been shot at before;
but they do not ignore,
that death is the wages of sin.

Some day they'll go down together
they'll bury them side by side.
To few it'll be grief,
to the law a relief
but it's death for Bonnie and Clyde.

Suicide Sal

We each of us have a good "alibi"
For being down here in the "joint"
But few of them really are justified
If you get right down to the point.

You've heard of a woman's glory
Being spent on a "downright cur"
Still you can't always judge the story
As true, being told by her.

As long as I've stayed on this "island"
And heard "confidence tales" from each "gal"
Only one seemed interesting and truthful-
The story of "Suicide Sal".

Now "Sal" was a gal of rare beauty,
Though her features were coarse and tough;
She never once faltered from duty
To play on the "up and up".

"Sal" told me this tale on the evening
Before she was turned out "free"
And I'll do my best to relate it
Just as she told it to me:

I was born on a ranch in Wyoming;
Not treated like Helen of Troy,
I was taught that "rods were rulers"
And "ranked" as a greasy cowboy.

Then I left my old home for the city
To play in its mad dizzy whirl,
Not knowing how little of pity

It holds for a country girl.

There I fell for "the line" of a "henchman"
A "professional killer" from "Chi"
I couldn't help loving him madly,
For him even I would die.

One year we were desperately happy
Our "ill gotten gains" we spent free,
I was taught the ways of the "underworld"
Jack was just like a "god" to me.

I got on the "F.B.A." payroll
To get the "inside lay" of the "job"
The bank was "turning big money"!
It looked like a "cinch for the mob".

Eighty grand without even a "rumble"-
Jack was last with the "loot" in the door,
When the "teller" dead-aimed a revolver
From where they forced him to lie on the floor.

I knew I had only a moment-
He would surely get Jack as he ran,
So I "staged" a "big fade out" beside him
And knocked the forty-five out of his hand.

They "rapped me down big" at the station,
And informed me that I'd get the blame
For the "dramatic stunt" pulled on the "teller"
Looked to them, too much like a "game".

The "police" called it a "frame-up"
Said it was an "inside job"
But I steadily denied any knowledge
Or dealings with "underworld mobs".

The "gang" hired a couple of lawyers,
The best "fixers" in any mans town,
But it takes more than lawyers and money

When Uncle Sam starts "shaking you down".

I was charged as a "scion of gangland"
And tried for my wages of sin,
The "dirty dozen" found me guilty-
From five to fifty years in the pen.

I took the "rap" like good people,
And never one "squawk" did I make
Jack "dropped himself" on the promise
That we make a "sensational break".

Well, to shorten a sad lengthy story,
Five years have gone over my head
Without even so much as a letter-
At first I thought he was dead.

But not long ago I discovered;
From a gal in the joint named Lyle,
That Jack and his "moll" had "got over"
And were living in true "gangster style".

If he had returned to me sometime,
Though he hadn't a cent to give
I'd forget all the hell that he's caused me,
And love him as long as I lived.

But there's no chance of his ever coming,
For he and his moll have no fears
But that I will die in this prison,
Or "flatten" this fifty years.

Tommorow I'll be on the "outside"
And I'll "drop myself" on it today,
I'll "bump 'em if they give me the "hotsquat"
On this island out here in the bay...

The iron doors swung wide next morning
For a gruesome woman of waste,
Who at last had a chance to "fix it"

Murder showed in her cynical face.

Not long ago I read in the paper
That a gal on the East Side got "hot"
And when the smoke finally retreated,
Two of gangdom were found "on the spot".

It related the colorful story
Of a "jilted gangster gal"
Two days later, a "sub-gun" ended
The story of "Suicide Sal".

Bibliography

Barrow, Blanche Caldwell and John Neal Phillips. My Life with Bonnie and Clyde. (Norman: University of Oklahoma Press, 2004.)

Burrough, Bryan. Public Enemies. (New York: The Penguin Press, 2004.)

Friedman, Lester D., Bonnie and Clyde. (BFI Publishing. 2000.)

Guinn, Jeff. Go Down Together: The True, Untold Story of Bonnie and Clyde. (New York: Simon & Schuster, 2009.)

Hinton, Ted & Grove Larry, Ambush; The Real Story of Bonnie and Clyde.

Knight, James R. and Jonathan Davis. Bonnie and Clyde: A Twenty-First-Century Update. (Austin, TX: Eakin Press, 2003.)

Milner, E.R. The Lives and Times of Bonnie and Clyde. (Carbondale and Edwardsville: Southern Illinois University Press, 1996.)

Nash, Jay Robert, Bloodletters and Badmen. (New York: M. Evans & Co., 1995.)

Parker, Emma Krause, Nell Barrow Cowan and Jan I. Fortune. The True Story of Bonnie and Clyde. (New York: New American Library, 1968.)

Penn, Arthur, Bonnie and Clyde. Edited by Lester D. Friedman. (Cambridge University Press. 2000.)

Phillips, John Neal. Running with Bonnie and Clyde, the Ten Fast Years of Ralph Fults. (Norman: University of Oklahoma Press, 1996, 2002)

Ramsey, Winston G., ed. On The Trail of Bonnie and Clyde. (London: After The Battle Books,

2003).

Steele, Phillip, and Marie Barrow Scoma. The Family Story of Bonnie and Clyde. (Gretna, LA: Pelican Publishing Company, 2000.)

Toland, John, The Dillinger Days. (New York: Random House, 1963.)

Treherne, John. The Strange History of Bonnie and Clyde. (New York: Stein and Day, 1984.)

Printed in Great Britain
by Amazon.co.uk, Ltd.,
Marston Gate.